TRUE FIGURES

TRUE FIGURES
Selected Shorter Poems and Prose Poems
1998–2021

David Blair

MadHat Press
Cheshire, Massachusetts

MadHat Press
PO Box 422, Cheshire MA 01225

Copyright © 2022 David Blair
All rights reserved

The Library of Congress has assigned
this edition a Control Number of
2022936429

ISBN 978-1-952335-41-9 (paperback)

Cover photo by Rebekah Modrak photograph from
her Re Made Co. multimedia intervention series.
Cover design by Robert J LeBlanc
Book design by MadHat Press

www.MadHat-Press.com

Published in the United States of America

Also by David Blair

2007

Ascension Days

2016

Friends with Dogs

Arsonville

2019

Walk Around: Essays on Poetry and Place

2020

Barbarian Seasons

*For Sabrina
& Astrid*

Table of Contents

One Day on the Vermont Border   1

I: Earlier

For George Romero   7
You Are So Beguiling   8
To William Morris   9
Cowardly Couplets   10
Sonnet for Robert Reich   11
Adventures in Moving   12
The Sneeksuck   13
The Return   14
About the Expatriate Jazz Musician Steve Lacy ...   15
Sound Solution ("*Die Spinnerin*")   16
Mirrors ("*Spiegel der Muse*")   17
About Songbooks   18
Election of the Saints   19
Lambs   20
Sonnet—to Central & Sacred Heart   21
Ode to *New Poems*   22
City Beach   23
I Vitelloni   24
Black Eyes   25

II: Peacefulness

Rosellini's *Flowers of Saint Francis*   29
Vinyl Raingear   30
At Park Street Station   31
Primitive   32
Mothership Prose   33
Stupidity Poem   34
Eighteen Blessed of the Dominican Order and Seventeen ...   35
In Peacefulness   36

Other *C'est Moi's* . . . 37
True Figures . . . 38
The Adorable Couple . . . 39
"In the middle of the night, it snowed" . . . 40
Lucy Days . . . 41
Doris Duke in Newport . . . 42
1900 Houses around Boston . . . 43
The Week of Bombs . . . 44
Vagrant Song—Boston Players . . . 46

III: Dog Days

Snorkels . . . 49
At Whole Foods . . . 50
Penned Horses . . . 51
Baroque Bodega . . . 52
In Philadelphia . . . 53
Away We Go . . . 54
Heart of Song . . . 55
Dr. Handball . . . 56
March Sky . . . 57
Poem about the Striking, Spatial Quality of Line . . . 58
Beach Blanket . . . 59
Girl with Dog . . . 60
Fiction Writers . . . 61
A Penguin John Donne . . . 62
Half Day . . . 63
Arethusa Savage . . . 64
Formal Feelings . . . 65
Gospel . . . 66
Lousy Person . . . 67
Poem about an Indian Restaurant Downtown . . . 68
Thor Ballylee by the Stream Heading Down . . . 69
Rabelais . . . 70
Drive-by Apostle . . . 71
Sonnet, Viking Funeral for a Workweek . . . 72

IV: Later

Is Writing Helpful?	75
Lines for Pope Francis in Cuba	76
Sadness	77
The Armies of Being Here	78
Somebody Was Believable	79
Problems with the Early Times Poetry	80
Sonnet for Older Fathers as Walter Matthau	81
For Dion in Belmont	82
Wanted Poster	83
My Mother's Depression	84
Black Mountain Music	85
For Goya's Public Ice Skaters of Spain	86
Eternal City	87

V: South Jersey

Seven Mile Beach	91
At the Cold Cut Table	92
In Monarch World	94
Acknowledgments	99
About the Author	101

One Day on the Vermont Border

A vetch—stairway to nowhere
with no lower steps—
and there is a lot to vetch about,
various femurs and forearms
and tibias of loose-skinned birches
in the scattered body of ferns
gone up into the hill country
the way the eye travels along
spines of an ankle-high vetch,
the broken pattern of the leaves
held by an arching stem,
absurd plant, pokiness, car trip
with dark glasses on
and passing the same barn
the color of squeezed teabags, twice.

*I don't want to leave out the euphoria
of the target shooters' burping reports,
the bikes with fat wheels abuzz
driven by the riders of snowmobiles,
on dirt roads in the woods
where mosquitos saw air
if you stop, the open and closed garages,
hoping that is not really a white pine
but a tower to bring phones back online
while we furiously wave our hands
in front of our faces, eating the bugs
more and more like ourselves by the yard.*

Even so, in all that blue and green,
nobody will be there
to stand in the sheds
by the coolers full of eggs
and asparagus gathered
from the meadow,
especially around big rocks,
dolmens nobody throws
in rivers and creeks,
and the coolers
are empty in the sheds
of these passive-aggressive types.

I. Earlier

For George Romero

The poor don't shoot their zombies
in the heads. Not in your version.
The zombies do the right things
horribly: the man mourned
embraces his wife. Then he bites
her shoulder. And then they go
ice skating, but without skates.

You Are So Beguiling

You are so beguiling
in the brown light
of pines, in your
new orange bathing suit,
the birds fall out
of the sky into your
flower pots when you come
back from the woods,
and when you bathe
in the low river,
even the sick shad
falls in love with you,
rosy and humid and lithe,
and swims under your ass
while you crouch in the river
which is otherwise unhealthy.

To William Morris

LADY ALICE:
Will you infect me?

SIR GUY:
Rest easy, maid.
I will infect you tonight.

LADY ALICE:
Will you infect another
as you journey forth?

SIR GUY:
My journey is long.
And I have but small legs.
Yet I shall infect.
I shall infect you again.

Cowardly Couplets

Some glimpses of the self bound across rocks in flocks, Edward Lear
self-caricatures, rounded quails, long stick legs, bespectacled vermin

in pizza shops at night, creatures that look up over their shoulders angry,
entirely projected, yet still holding out the manifold knives you describe.

Sonnet for Robert Reich

Somebody odd who loved him toted twenty pounds
of dried rabbit chow through the subway turnstiles
when election defeats melted into drug store carpets
headed to scrubbers and sponges, cosmetics, sink stuff
and Mr. Peanut on his cane, tilting his urbane body skull
at all the ungovernableness, at former secretary Reich
and his tall wife crossing my path through Cambridge,
seeming decent and happy. Somebody small-mouthing
an Anjou pear with thin lips made health and life measly,
strictly for the rabbits. Put your hands under his arms,
man who would be governor, and lift him up in a light
that melts stubborn icicles, that creates a special tan,
that wedges bits of cotton between toes at the pedicurist,
that arranges old womanly hair into tinfoil chicken wings.

Adventures in Moving

I'll speak like an older brother parroting the words
of an older cousin. No warm remove is too warmly removed
for you. Beware of the doddering, semi-suburban drivers
on their short legs up the turnpike. Beware of these
stingy-brimmed straw fedoras. In general beware of drivers
who wear hats at all. I know that the comfort of what I can say
exists independently of what can be said, a utilities shed
on the edge of the woods, a cow's great tongue
near the muddy lip of the waterhole and chicory. Beware.

The Sneeksuck

This is a smalltime megalith.
This is earth's hat stand.
The stone house is Neolithic
where the brook drains leaves,
some sort of ice age shanty.

I don't believe in wearing any getup.
Things you do with rocks can be more
comforting than things done with mud.

Creep into the stone house.
A snake sucks some eggs
and has the small flag of food.

The idea of lasting is dented;
some junk won't burn up or inclines that way.

The Return

I was glad I wasn't a shoe
on Washington Street,
and then white shawls and habits
at the cashiers inspected
my mirrors and tags,
brisk, exotic nun hands darting,
and Russian ladies tried me on
all Saturday afternoon in the basement.

Then traveled back from bedroom carpets,
the lady's can at the Hyatt,
booze cruised, done almost in,
done almost in by null house music.
Shoes think, *Boris doesn't love me anymore.*
Shoes would go to Reno if they could.

Little shoe theater, tarted up pumps,
high-heeled sandals, filigreed,
filamentous boots, so many shoes
like cake, so many inedible,
perversely angled and matted
as our malicious makers who draft
us one by one at sloped tables
behind gold leaf lettered windows
across the alley from the sweatshop.

About the Expatriate Jazz Musician Steve Lacy, after Seeing Portraits of Han-shan and Shi-te

Others may hold the scroll, you
may have the broom, loony sage,
bath water just right now,
and you roll around in that
which is your homely broom.
Steve Lacy looks like some detective
retirement cardigan, Palm Springs,
balding from porkpies,
grandpa admittance, lonesome
applications and reaches: soprano sax,
Detective Steve Lacy, Paris
gendarme, golfs a bit, goofs
the hotel setting, the disappointed
raspberry sauce off the cake plates
all the long table wants to scrape at,
fork at, prolong,
so the long table files out
like 7th inning at Dodger Stadium
that misses how to live here.

Sound Solution ("*Die Spinnerin*")

As I spilled sand on the rug and stood in bare feet,
a young person trotted around me with a jetpack.
I missed my ping-pong paddle, all of my hair,
and the entire cut of the record. Rueful. Had life
all gone by me in lines? The needle oaks tipped over,
their roots as wide as their tops. If you make soup
in a Weber kettle, soup puts out the glowing coals,
a swindle involving sour clouds. But with nuns
and tree-houses, sun-stitched as an oak convent in branches,
as a fish in the bleachers, melting, not burning, the book,

the room was still as finely spun material.
Come now, you know the ranges
can sign endlessly the tall dome.

Mirrors ("*Spiegel der Muse*")

Wanting to deck you or herself out, she was looking at running waters for her reflection to steady, but waters were moving quickly. It was raining. There are times when you get ready this uncertainly yourself. No wonder that your partner in this enterprise is the same way: trying to figure out the place to begin and the place to end up in the accelerations of time. All the possible places are too vague. There is no way to want to go out anywhere when you are dressed for nowhere in particular. Cool night waits in the plush seat of the car with the motor running in the rain until finally it is steakhouse weather, and there are unreflective settings.

About Songbooks

Let's get clear of what could be set for piano or mezzo-soprano.
Sometimes the mirrors in the cushion fall away, peaks in the water
catching, and moonlight on fast running water throws up sparks.
Aside from roundness, the moon has a speaking voice; everybody loves
roundness and round sounds. There used to be beloved hams
in America, bearded actors, fat and gray, character players
in morning coats and tuxedo shoes. When I was a morning paperboy
on Shady Avenue, I used to look up at the morning stars and deliver
and feel hopeless. I think that loss would be like going back in time
in the worst way possible. Road images discourage. Burnt corks of mirage
at the peaks of every next inclination on the turnpike just remind me
that traveling towards you is getting both away from myself and back
at myself if I imagine myself to be a place that I wouldn't stop or be from.
Nor do I imagine your voice to be anything remotely like ceaselessly weary
ocean routines. I don't think of you or feel near you by the water
much especially in a way to build on if you were truly an absent horizon
past the airport, an eyeful of empty beyond the rocks and harbor boats.
The sky ruled out, the water no help, already knowing that the road would
be useless, I would rather not speak or even think through things at all.

Election of the Saints

Traveling through the landscape
of election signs,
did you ask, *Who is he?*
and *Who is he?*
and *Who is he?* of names
held aloft at intersections,
on fresh pine stakes
in yards? When you tell
me how your mother ran
out of gas on purpose,
so the two of you would
walk along the lavender
medians and across
the margins of pine
along the road, I imagine
loving a person in his faults
or hers: allowing the car
to run out of gas, gladly,
to stop driving and walk.

Lambs

People come out of the seemingly residential building
where the psychoanalysts still are for now
part of the order of lunch and commercial transactions.
And that's good. Sad times though
when after this he gets barred from a flower shop
where they won't let him buy dried poppies again,
which he would carry through the evening
to a date with an interior decorator
who needs the skeletal nodes for a vase.
Some parts of him are out on the streetcar lines
and feel like Montreal with all the Russians
and walk-up mesmerists.
He won't make the mistake of telling
curbside beggar kids he is sorry.
They don't believe people
and would whine junk-sick curses to Vancouver
if only there were a smaller continent underneath,
the way penned blond sheep move together
or a single sheep dances with a child in a field
as green as mint jelly under clouds of mutton fat jade.

Sonnet—to Central & Sacred Heart

As slow, as inexorable, a sort of bee made of rain eating a canal
along the curve of a pear, mourning any beautiful orchards
into a vast house of hieroglyphics: even so I am not listening
to golden notes that could be skimming just above the waters
with their mouths open, the terns diving by the pools. Hawks circle
at the last inlet on the Jersey cape then. Out in back of apartments,
an unheated indoor porch, paint buckets with their sloppy lips
and metal handles rusting are part of doubling up in life, the festival.
At swine-fests and churchgoing, everybody gets their crackling festivity.
I almost forgot about my dream of cremation, buildings in cemeteries,
not just the airbrushed sides on a van, sword fights down the winding
castle wings. Hands that have sewn patches on denim jackets, smelling
of rain, cigarette smoke, my stoned brothers, other astringents roughly
blooded with damp cotton balls, what's it like to drink fresh breast milk?

Ode to *New Poems*

The snow gathered in rocks and moats. These red clouds
shut the sun off in bricks. Their strange skins replaced
our short, furred ears, too. Suppers sloshed in buckets.

Dunk sticky Rilke translators in the murky tank of seals.
Keep the town line folded in your pocket, discarded necktie.

Park birds turned crazed flocks back and forth at the ruffle
of the brown hawk's wingspan. It was a good time to avoid
the decent zero's division, but lion ears grew soft at it.

City Beach

Barrooms empty and too much parking along the low concrete wall
    to breakers,
the horizon itself a form of immaculate meanness: cloud-shadows in
    the sand
like old tattoos, and also at the bar, these gentleman who have saved
    the elegance
of their cruelty, their appreciative airs, certified public loafers,
    dancehall lechers,
too slender for the sea, too wiry for wealth, dull eyed as sharks,
    these habitués.

And the manager of the restaurant that extends into the bay says that
    the ghosts
and demons are coming up through the floorboards, what gangster
    craft docks
at the end of the short pier, what hearts will explode, and losses
    continue to mount
until seagulls and people trade places on the hard dirty cake, past
    pine-fringed rocks
and causeway roads to spice islands and velvet socialites conked out
    on the john floor.

I Vitelloni

The lobsters were sending click code to each other in their paper bag
and tasted of sweat socks once they were cooked
far from the idea of the capitol, which was like a lit runway
seen from outlying areas, from hills and palisades and shoreline.
It was down to the hour when all the signs come on
with a storm pack coming in from the northwest.
Some old cats had slices of pizza by the January seawall in their
    Cadillac.
The teenaged lovers were getting fluorescent, but had found themselves
and circled about each other on the sand littered with paper cups
    and napkins
while it whipped in ankle-high sand ribbons towards the pale green
    water.
When these two kids opened their coats to each other, they saw the
    skyline far away—
but there were also these men milling around, driving themselves crazy.
Each one of them pulled his cafe blazer and tie against the thaw ending
among empty benches. The steps down from the seawall were obscured
    by sand.

Black Eyes

September, 2001

The heavy lacquered frames of the grannies and grand dames
    of Cadillac and Pontiac and El Dorado
and the summer highways are my own white-walled wheels and red
    detailing
and baby's butt white leather interiors

and have kept me from peripheral vision, kept me in black eyes,
my head in a beehive and a yellow jacket,
my tomatoes in a brown paper bag,
three kingly sunflowers
spitting their teeth in the mud,
in the sunlight which was black night,
funneled me in black lenses,
sweet country vision, sweet strangeness.

If you were black marble
in a public square, men and women would wade the fountains
to kiss down your inner thigh to instep arch,
sweet strangeness, sweet country vision.

The waterfront sent seal calls and caulked groans,
the echoes of docked boats rubbed out on the sides of piers.
It wasn't right, the waterfront hotels and the privacy of boats
where the drinkers of gin wore life vests.
Out in points of weeds, there were benches
and rusted ladders out of the harbor.
The drainage of the sky split the spaces
between loud party boats where sounds
swallowed themselves in black water.

II. Peacefulness

Rosellini's *Flowers of Saint Francis*

Brother Chico. Brother Marx. Brother Brother.
Physical sadness is physical immensity in exertion,
pleasure burning, a stairwell that winds and winds.
Barefoot in cold rain gets hit by sticks
or hit by cattlemen. There's a Mormon on a daisy
margin in composed lighting. Hit him.
The harshness of life is made sweet
by companionship, coin of the realm.
Praise that poverty now.

Vinyl Raingear

With all these feathering maple flowers and oaks, this driving the streets
has all the eventual bad health of hillbilly music or the French New Wave
as some watery Cambridge people in sudden parks have shed Talbots
and Anne Bradstreet straight lines and fleecy bundles for sundresses
and low-riders to show their fire-fangled tattoos on lower bare backs
rule Britannia, rule the waves. In the middle there is light-splashed tang
of the street with the bus not there yet.
                                          The next day is a sad one,
it's winter again. Some people are to their sandals as some hikers
are to bad weather in the mountains: caught out. The rain whips up.
Umbrellas gleam over pedestrians with tight cake boxes and aspirations
and daughters or nieces or kid sisters able to hold two light items in a bag—
Seaside lady traveling with your ward from the Foodmaster, bring me
      to your Foodmaster.

At Park Street Station

A season of beautiful raincoats
and squirrel phones,

their haircuts, skirts, and suits
always better looking,

to relationship negotiations
and other quail feathers,

dinner plates,
work stuff, couples

carry on their heavy work
the way the coyotes hold anvils,

the subway on one level,
slim streetcars up here,

walls, ceilings, tunnels
sprayed with fire repellant,

against fire, but not mud,
catacombs, a Venetian future.

Isn't it romantic,
and won't it be?

Yes, and yes.

Primitive

Uncanny—the little shrine our friend
Tanya's grandfather built around his Virgin Mary statue,
lawnchairs pointed at it, a stone in each chair—maybe for the souls
of great-grandparents—in New Jersey, where Walt Whitman lived
like a long-horned sheep in a meadow
wedged as a paper stopper for elderberry wine.

Mothership Prose

Where is the boss? Maybe Vermont. As for the boss under that boss, I give up on Fridays in July.

May the cruise ship of these hours, depopulated summer, come in with white shorts and crisp white shirts and even more clavicles.

I am about to step into the golden assistance of late afternoon where the bicycles with training wheels and lacrosse sticks will be out on quiet streets.

Except for these tubes of fluorescent light, the moment is like the one right before I step up the stairs from one dark floor to another to bed.

There are times when I fall face forward into the fast moving streams where my dirty shoes have again filled up with water, silt, and warm fish.

These streams are like one of those places in the wilderness where my size twelve feet can actually be in all three mountain state at once.

Stupidity Poem

I am not a golden superhero,
but my boot is a superhero.

Eighteen Blessed of the Dominican Order and *Seventeen Blessed of the Dominican Order and Two Dominican Tertiaries*

With chin and beak, according to Fra Angelico
finches and swallows come out of the dazzle
for hacked birdseed and suet on the gold.

In Peacefulness

In peacefulness, true. They were choosing paint just like two dream countries. Denying each other foodstuffs once in a while, every once in a while moving some stuff around, shooting some stuff.

Other *C'est Moi's*

> *"Madame Bovary, c'est moi."*

Little fellahin named Bruno, *c'est moi*,
a calla lily, health store carob, okay,
bald publisher, gardens, apples, pears,
diabetic former drinkers
of homemade wine, all that, c'est moi, plus
the whole concept of Fabrizio
in *The Charterhouse at Parma*, of course.
Parents are running a three-legged race
no matter what. The crinkly
clusters settle on the leaves
as if left by indigent moths
who only want state flowers.
The state flower, that's me,
prolonged natural
contrary movements.
It's hurricane season,
and the neighbors have been half-naked
since Easter Monday.
Time to fly into fast-moving oaks
as if to chew gum
and eat walnuts at once.
The ladies folding laundry
have boxer shorts
on their heads—
political comedy
or patrimony.

True Figures

That one is like an initial independent clause when Ulysses S. Grant says how some captain got decapitated.

The Adorable Couple

In the bar, she shouts back, I'M A MUSIC THERAPIST. Small bar, the musicians stand between the customers, and that's from a plunger, that trumpet mute. I WORK IN PALLIATIVE CARE. The magnolias are all brown shreds because they bloomed too early. I AM A HOSPICE PHYSICIAN. What do people want to hear on your guitar? WISE MEN KNOW. ONLY FOOLS FALL IN LOVE. The door opens. Cold air. Soporific, early spring, burning, cold.

I WENT TO A CHRISTIAN COLLEGE IN BUCKS COUNTY, IN PENNSYLVANIA.

These two, their bedroom is a flute case. No.

I PLAY FOUR SETS A DAY. GUITAR. LOVE SONGS. HYMNS. FOR PEOPLE WHO ARE DYING.

"In the middle of the night, it snowed"

In the middle of the night, it snowed.

There was moisture in the air all winter that never got cold, and in the middle of the air there was a crossing guard in a florescent green coat, double wide.

There was a boulder with a turnip on top of it under miles of clouds. There was a tattoo shop in the foggy glow. Seagulls in the parking lot: a whole lot of cotton wadding.

If you would only remove your surgical mask, I could see that kisser.

Lucy Days

I am sorry
for feigning
personhood
so many times
before I was one.

The sun falls
on the grass
poking snow,
kind of irritating,

the directions
also absurd,
high-pleated
archaic fat man pants,

to make us walk
like Fred Mertz
until it hurts.

Doris Duke in Newport

Despite my most general political
feeling for the big Bellevue eyesores,
there is a strange cheerful sense
of spirit—maybe it is mine—

at Rough Point, mansion
museum of Doris Duke,
keeper of pet camels,
friend of Martha Graham,
Malcolm Forbes,
jazz musicians,
Imelda Marcos.

Where the footbridge is
down at the front of her mansion's
seaside backyard
for the Cliff Walk,
you see a cave full of ocean.
That H. H. Richardson
knew his stuff—
it's a portal, a parable
of ownership.
There is power
but not ownership.

You can get the same thing
from a merry-go-round
or if you run through vineyard rows
with a glass of wine after your child,
or if you look through an egret's legs.

1900 Houses around Boston

The unaccountable dead are involved
in your domestic concord and disputes.
Another reveals the hard plastic gnomes
in the garden with the yellow hosta leaves
loped over on them
when you think of the lady whose garden gnomes
they once were. They break a measuring cup.
The record player starts up. It's freaky.

The dead are great surveillance.

Did you think
my mom would check up on me at school?
And the good news is that no matter
what they were before, the dead are socialists.
All these thoughts and travesties seem to float
above my head as if yellow locust leaves
the size of fingernails flew upwards
and could just be there somehow
borne on magic jets of my paranoia.

The Week of Bombs

I tell my friend anything on Beacon.

That I found 1983 beach novels so sexy
with embossed letters and vertical cracks,
the alphabet of love, for horn dog kids.

That I freak out all night about different things
and feel glad that the birds make a racket.

Days after the bomb, we drive around town
and are still hopeless sad jokers,
still starting a strange momentum.

W. C. Fields is still funny. Og Oggilby is.
The whole look of cowboy boots
and sundresses seems good for the human spirit.

I remember a lady who put one boot on a trunk
and pulled her dress over head
with practically no hands.
Her boots were blue
and her hair was brown.

I would rather lose one arm
than a leg, but would take two
arms over two legs. Who gets to choose?

The talk, the actions, the deeds, the desires
are all that remain, the important stuff.
The glove compartment is a good idea.

To say otherwise is a demonstration.

Vagrant Song—Boston Players

Saturday night, the white Lord & Taylor still open,
and the modern wing of the library had driven aground
its white hull into pedestrian space—its only cramped spree
in the restaurants rubbed away by suburban pleasure-seekers
and conventioneers and college students, those who greet eyes
and the returners of stares, the Morse code of the antennae
on top of the buildings—men, women, women, men, women,
women, men, men, men, women, women—under heat-lamps
over strong under-wires uplifting and proffering more bread
and awnings of sudden hotels, in whose dark shine a river coils
black and colder than the crushed ice, clams, lobsters, bottles,
up through the cobalt parking space of each monk's bright cell
that subdivides wall-less floors of the concrete parking towers,
basic and beautiful buildings, unpretentiously for the night.

"Your body is a paradise/ your body is a paradise," a vagrant
shook his cup by the Symphony 7-11. After another knock-out
the big conductor, you can say, had great small feet, rolling
quickly on the high stool. He left the stage like a champ,
holding both hands up in the air to the side of his head.
You could hear a rattle of dice somewhere in there,
ghost players on a phantom train. So many violin players
were in the bushes. The young ladies with their cellos
were wide open to the music. Backstage, oboists were cranking
salsa and hip hop, playing grab-ass, snapping jocks and ties.

III. Dog Days

Snorkels

People who have intelligence in love,
the people I love best in the world, the smart ones,
have the same big bug-eyes and face masks as ants

for snorkeling, a beautiful black ant nature.
I don't worry that I will be eaten by labs.
Their heads are all brains inside crisp vinyl.

What with their brains and their giant eyes,
they seem curious as cats,
cats who are not cats
but generosities.

Maybe all the Norse gods want to kill
that which lives by water and rock
and by the borders, the damp regions.

Watch out if you live near the jetties.

With a donkey, you have to follow
eye contact with cautious handfuls of hay,
and things can be tenebrous for some time.

At Whole Foods

How orderly is this shopping
scene here after work:
the pebbles of the stream
get smooth, touched only
by salamander fingers and toes.
We had burrs in our tube socks.
There are so many delicious
looking people here. I am afraid
they are the ground turkey.
Or maybe just one of us
will be thrown out of here
any minute. Hopefully
not me. Think fast:
black-eyed Susans come up
in high grass, calm moths.
The last horsehead oil pump
in Pennsylvania
needs WD-40. A string
of city kids on a daytrip
are on the approach.
It looks shadow-colored
from down the road
but orange, blazoned, up close.

Live crawdad, you are just a lung.

Penned Horses

I could identify at once with the horses out on the old post road,
near swamps, by stonewalls, by ice-cream shacks, the horses eating
with rubbery, fingering lips, which are outright, forthright and creeping,
while captive sheep stood around making a sound like *wuuuu, wuuuuu.*

This all still goes on out here. The two rural teenagers visit the horse cafeteria
and hold out handfuls of grass for them to eat, and kiss them and scratch them,
so pleasing to the gay horses and the straight horses and the bisexual ones, too.

The horses turn their heads sideways to receive these kindly benedictions
and quote heartbreaker lyrics to themselves and use a lot of their quiet
to communicate what tenderness and humor they feel in the situation.

Baroque Bodega

The ground-beef empanadas are, first of all, saintly in a baroque church niche carving sort of way downstairs at the bodega, golden diapers.

Got it. Potted meat in dusty cans, and there is a cardboard box of fuses so don't explode, not with a lot of syrupy-looking cleaning supplies, sponges, beer, the kinds of coffee you really should make, salami, the tabloids.

I believe I am painted in egg white and a tree frog.

In Philadelphia

Somewhere, the glue sticks are baking, growing molten, filling tubes, being sliced. The skies are full of disgusting chemical smoke.

If you spent the night in the police station across the street, I don't really know that I should front you carfare to Abington.

There are not many people who work in the factory, pushing buttons to operate the enormous buckets, shears, conveyor belts, and they all have autoimmune diseases, pattern baldness, weakened teeth.

The mid-Atlantic region has an upset stomach and cramps.

Away We Go

Maybe a year before she was really sick, part of her mouth was stiff for about five days, as she had a minor growth removed or a temporary palsy.

Heart of Song

I think I might be a folk song when I hear one sung by an artist.

    An old folk singer strikes a pose
strong-looking standing semi-bowlegged, pretends to like strength.

Nobody really does. The unspoken in every lyric might be baloney.

Dr. Handball

Nothing to do with a teen body pulled from the Nile but row the boat of its mummy for hieroglyphs on pyramids and handball courts, murals, painted, peeling "in Memory of Mush" off Bathgate Avenue,

being a handball pro with an identity and legend, for money, money,

so maybe can go around the world, when your arm is a catapult to shape the air in the bluing light where we will play by sound alone, slow and old Greek generals catching a break.

Midnight Dragon. You can roll with the Midnight Dragon, its ontological argument, its eerie remnants.

March Sky

I just thought I was talking to somebody who also had a dream and that we could talk because we understood something about the circus.

We were watching Dutch clouds over Dutch ships over Dutch waves, the variances of steeliness and fixity.

That was the exact street corner.

Poem about the Striking, Spatial Quality of Line

Same as these porcelain salt shakers shaped like upright hogs, this is all sturdy enough to be out in the pine barrens on a picnic with sun-faded green denim over all utensils and tools, snapped mess kits, canteens.

Do we stop or are we stopped by great lines? The best parts are the places where you can not pedal past them anymore, but wet cedars invent the idea of cedar chips, and the vines have hairy bark.

Lean your bicycle against a tree.

Beach Blanket

The fact is people are surprisingly simple, so they do simple things like shell beans, drink gimlets in summer, slice tomatoes for white bread, pull weeds.
Go on into space, build deer hunting stands in the branches of posted woods, compose ring cycles from rose dust, cobble together long family sagas, too.
That way, we not only prepare for global catastrophe but can get over shocking boredom.

Corky people drink corky red wine, in corky shoes, with flower garlands swirling in the foam.

Girl with Dog

Going around Lake Ponkapoag, there were these two kinds of dancers—our six-year-old and your good dog.

for Peter

Fiction Writers

Maybe I really should get paranoid. Who do you sound like? You walk by the veterans hall one night in June.

You see the evergreen Christmas garlands pinned up by the drop ceiling tiles because the windows are open. Everything has a story, crazy.

Brown olive drab helmets, holsters, gasmasks, handguns, and rifles—are those machine gun belts?—just lit up a case, far side of the blue pool table lamp, maybe relics of some nut.

Because the door is open. Because you make stuff up.

All sorts of people live around here, high rent, ragged cuffs, dirty looking, good chow.

for Keith Lee

A Penguin John Donne

There were agreeable and disagreeable distances of primary and secondary and tertiary, celestial and terrestrial regions in his ruff.

Half Day

In winter, no birds, no basketballs, and then it's birds and basketballs, and I'm relieved.

I love to be alone, I hate it.

When I was a kid, I loved to go on the bus and see Pittsburgh, alone. I don't mind getting the alone in me, once I get going.

When I am alone, I am happy.

The kids come out of the school, skirted with short shadows, the basketball courts lined with branch shadows. Is that a tremble in the air of radiator heat in these windows or cold out there?

It is like driving from New York, a weekday expanse.

Arethusa Savage

The brown Frankenstein Cliffs in Crawford Notch State Park look like the color photo of Cold Mountain, China, on the cover of the Red Pine translation of Han Shan, but the Arethusa Falls are in a savage amphitheater of Canadian bathing suits and a crêche of broken trunks.

Formal Feelings

After great pain, it's like daylight savings time, sudden, squint-worthy,
    tired-eyed.
If bugs had mammal brains, they would feel formal heading for the
    cracks and walls.

Who put all these trees here,
and then soil, bulbs sending up their hard,
automatic mixers,

so I can't wait for moonlight on bodega red awning?

for Katie

Gospel

If somebody has died on you, be careful of the best.

Don't listen to Sam Cooke and the Soul Stirrers.

All the lyrics are about the importance of death in any kind
    of actual life.

Don't play the music of every sort of ambiguity.
There is embarrassment there and professionalism.

for David Rivard

Lousy Person

Being kind of lousy, he thinks, "Maybe it's you not listening to me." Some palpable realm of sunshine above his mind, that kind of reader.

Poem about an Indian Restaurant Downtown

The fewer the details, the more universal the figure of lunch.

Stepped on sidewalk cellar doors eaten away by rust. And then glass blocks lit somehow with some of them smashed. Eating lunch alone in an almost empty buffet—the fewer the diners, the denser tandoori chicken, the turmeric.

Some people leave you all alone with breads. I am one of the people who do that. Yet I complain too. The sweeter the mango, the more salt on my lips and pakora.

Late snow falling into crocuses and in between daffodil leaves and stems on the street, and in the garden, and on the common. The fewer the details, the more you cartoon. The blue god sits bare-chested and vested among the gopi; blue, the people on their way through the park.

Thor Ballylee by the Stream Heading Down

Saw a bird in the stream seem to play the stone with its tail-feather.
Quiet, nobody around, the center closed, I didn't want to leave

the scaly backyard silver birches,
white-faced cows looking over the gate
across the road on the other side of the bridge.
Did Yeats drive? Astrid handed me a branched stick
shaped like a broken Y while we crawled around the wood,
the best five-year-old ever. I didn't want to leave
the noisy quiet. Sea-green slates are okay with me,
everything to go down underground from the turlough.

Rabelais

I don't mind if people talk about actual shit
because life is earthy.

Out of mud, comes the brick.
Out of earth, our friends come,
giant in aspect, like Thomas Andrew Yuill,
the poet from Old Dominion.

"Yoo hoo," he says. "Read more Wyatt. Read
Sir Philip Sidney."
"Yoo hoo," he says. "Buttermilk biscuits.
Gravy. Monday Night Football."

"Yoo hoo," he says. "The heart is gold."

Greet the day.

Drive-by Apostle

Because of the guardrail where the highway goes
    over the lakes of central Massachusetts,
two fishermen stand on water, not on a boat,
for two thousand years, abra-ca-hocus,
metal tablets shot up on the imaginary
    tribal names, the little preppies.
    Everything that happens
these disaster days
disproves solitary fates.

Sonnet, Viking Funeral for a Workweek

After work, I put my foot on the edge of the weekdays
and give them a shove back out into the harbor as I stand
on this rotting wood which doesn't float so much as it rolls
and bumps like a shopping cart smashed out of the parking lot
by a truck full of frozen carrots and peas. The old Sikh
ladies maybe couldn't really stand fast grabby grandsons
in the aisles where nobody noticed if less pampered kids—
girls—fell off the whale-watch pontoon boat that bounced
back in from the algae-rich feeding grounds near the shore.
Friday night is on already when a guy cuts by wearing dark
brown pants and a light brown dress shirt and coffee-colored
pointy shoes. I shoot the boat with my burning arrows of love.
I salute you as you disappear, lazy porpoises, dear students,
with all of your pigtails, your tattooed faces, your sloppy hearts.

IV. Later

Is Writing Helpful?

> *hellish bullshit ... men love it*
> *men stupid as cows, pigs*
> —Ikkyu (Berg)

After telling each other
some awful stuff, the three of us
were poking along Houghton Street.

Then, wow, there were grapes
and a tan Cadillac sedan like a bubble
parked under a trellis, dim in darkness.

And we stood there in the dimness,
smoking cigarettes and enjoying
the jam smell, all September buzzed.

Then somebody got in that car,
turned on the lights,
drove away. Where to?

Lines for Pope Francis in Cuba

That scene in *The Leopard* when the family goes to mass
and sits up front alongside the altar in high-backed wood,

but now this—

that nun who is young for a Cuban nun
in a brown habit like a cigar wrapper sings,

that big band orchestra of Cardinals in red beanies
about to stand up and swing that music behind the pope,

that country, we keep a jail there,
that damp closet, we like the sandwich,

that country that is so close and so far away
and is perhaps shaped a bit like kidneys or livers,

that old scholar who seems beyond grading people
and thinking he is some sort of big-time standard,

that space they made for the priests and nuns in wheelchairs,
that sense of hot, of tropical hot, and antique standing fans.

Sadness

I remember you were the one there
standing by me, smiling with me.

Your cat, your dog, that pain,
sings, "Rescue me." Always.

When I walk by
the Armory castle,

I have to guard
the Armory castle.

The word *ugh*
gets to be a word, too.

The stuttering, happy breaths of a dreaming girl,
even a nine-year-old. Out in the sky,

someone sleeps, someone, someone sleeps.

Some beautiful person leaned out, rang
a bell out a window after making it creak,

                        casting a spell
on the night and the neighborhood and you.
It wasn't a raccoon. She was opening a window.

The Armies of Being Here

Maybe a college graduate or a student,
chunky clubby on hands and knees
squirts tasty bleach on the pedestals
of her exercise job purgatory
as if a boxer aimed his spit
at the gym floor
where Montgomery Clift
as Pvt. Robert E. Lee Prewitt
with spacy demented eyes
kept plucking dandelion violets
from the floors of physical health
where people bring their sad bodies,
and cell phones, and the half-employed
get their euphoria and their yas yas out.

Somebody Was Believable

Somebody was believable, Olive Oyl. At the farmer's market,
so many arms with permanent tattoo schmutz on them,
part of me will always think, out-of-tune and step.

Problems with the Early Times Poetry

Out with yard stars and the ragged tomatoes in coffins, the big houses and the grills throw smoke. Eat the whole grill, why don't you? Big country. We all loved younger poets. Let me tell you of the early days when the settlers lived in these log cabins and did nothing but make Alpo. They were writing folksy love poems. They were smearing Chia Pet seed all over the terra-cotta sculptures of Yoda. They missed the path through the dunes and wound up in the dunes with some biting brown flies and then pricked by cactuses and dune grass with secretive sawtooth edges. They filled housefuls with heads in the rain, piling creative anachronism shields and swords made from black foam wrapped in silver duct tape. Their beards and their armpits smelled like green lentils cooked with smoked ham hocks. There were hordes, and they lived cheap, but they slept late.

Sonnet for Older Fathers as Walter Matthau

I went to some parties that didn't work, and other
places our heads go, fields named for bankers, hard
cracked infield dirt, no rakes. The tennis courts
lit up at night, and we drove by exciting night tennis
in the city. We were encased in white polyester
baseball pants. The shirts were awful orange.
Who gets to be the fat catcher? Me. Sometimes,
a family tyrant sucked all the world into an angry
orange balloon. We loved dumb movies because
they got us. Somebody had to get us. I remember
a drinker with a pool who cursed and scared us
all. And our parents could be grouches but never
brought us to that bug-zapper, bad suburban place
again, and never just said anyone was that plain nuts.

For Dion in Belmont

The Napoleons got theatrical.
The bakery surrounded me with cakes
years after when I got along
with an invisible transistor

and getting called Hey-Boom-Boom-Washington, nice hat, ah,
    walk on.
Dull bronze eggs of peppermint-striped string dispensers hung
    on chains
level with a modish clock built into the paneling above an egress.
I saw snowy egrets by the dump on the edge of Pelham Bay Park.
    The hunt.

And in a dark night the bread-only bakery was open and windowless,
its doorframe full of bare bulbs, no fluorescence, and the crust
would rivulet into floury cracks,

the gush that swells and dissolves
with traces of peppery dust, fresh.
In the morning, the girls had nail extensions
with glue-on rhinestones on them like spaceships.

Wanted Poster

In all the blab
and pork chop
and love
and hate,
we need solitude
and silence, too.

My Mother's Depression

My mother liked the thirties, which she sort of remembered, boiling water and ketchup for automat soup, and her mother. You know what pissed her off? My brother peeing up at her face at diaper time in 1963. She could hold a grudge, keep an enemy, little orphan Ovaltine cup, arf, an old vase. It was from the DEPRESSION, thrown out, or not, nothing better than then.

Black Mountain Music

"The looseness of music,"
I start to say, but, uh, 10-4, negatory
on that comment. I stood ten feet
from a string quartet
and what I was feeling
about the violinist—so many
of these string sections
two elves and a big oaf
playing cello who looks like a cello—
my mind gone visiting Ben Shahns,
socialist realist oompah-loompahs,
the real short one named Nerdlia
from Romania, who stood
about five foot four
in her heels, big square
classical music heels,
I had to read all the program notes.

Tony Bennett says if he had done
nothing else but be a singing waiter
in Astoria, Queens,
he would have been all right,

just a singular voice.

For Goya's Public Ice Skaters of Spain

Mostly nothing between my mind and poem, I do
not regard the wet night that dries
away from the house on the rubber roof,
dry snow always a misnomer
as it chases itself there into and out of drifts
until the snow sticks. The town rink
keeps full of fascinating cold
from the hard shine of its oval
to the brown wooden rafters,
to the metal stands, the penalty boxes,
scoreboard box, team benches, cinderblock
walls that do not screen out the cold
with dreaming goons and figure eights,
to ads for insurance agents and dental smiles
and restaurants. I do not sharpen my skates.
I don't care if they look dude-like or femme
and never did, was always a dork, a shmoo.
I go slow, I keep upright, I sweat and ice over
at the same time, outside night, outside daytime,
surrounded by miniature figure skaters, blue tops,
hockey pucks, hoodlum-loompahs, the middle-aged
and the old, and teenagers who also remember
the rinks other places, all of them outdoors
in the snowflakes, sudden stars, nobody talented.

Eternal City

The only eternal city is the one people make of it. When there were hundreds of daily newspapers, including one in Latvian, nobody was young. There were no swimming pools in the hotels under mirrored ceilings. There was polio. The workers came home from the printing presses with broken necks. The women had burns on their fingers from wrapping the jaw-breaking Squirrel Nut Zippers while they were still hot taffies. In those days, I thought I had to decide whether to learn Hebrew, Greek or the tablets of the Mesopotamia. Instead, we learned to spot the burial mounds of the Hopewell civilization, right where it began, the beginning of bad luck for Hoosiers everywhere, and ending in limestone steps. Soldier's Field Road seems to take me towards the buildings of downtown Boston and away from them at once. Just as a solider seems to be growing old for one moment but is trapped forever at the end of youth, if I have to make a right turn to get there, how can the eternal city be straight ahead?

The past and future are unworthy of each other. That's how.

I would like to sit cross-legged across from you on the bed and remove your corn-colored hair extensions again.

V. South Jersey

Seven Mile Beach in October

Pulls the grate down on the bait shop, lumberjack shirt, time.
Before they go colors of hays, wetland cordgrasses burn green,

scraggly tree	of black-head	loudmouthed	gulls
all gone.	A lot	of loudmouths	gone.

Quiet, egrets hang around like old ballets, barroom full of treeless,
uniform afternoon shine. Then close your eyes on the bright beach.

Along the waves, dunlins shoot as black, headless vertebrae. Step in

Fred's Tavern,	the still	dark,	and still	dark.
Smells like	cola,	booze,	coco,	beer.

for Walt

At the Cold Cuts Table

Most cows *like* to be milked.
Some animals are really dull
as Canada geese
who nap, nip on the median.
The years go by too quickly
when I visit my aunt and uncle
for coffee, my silver-haired
aunt and uncle.

Sandwich time, we
all torture each other
around the kitchen table,
the mayo, the mustard,
the fathers and sons,
the moms, the cousins,
but the underhanded subtext
of meanness and competition
only flares out for a moment,
one note among many
notes flying and back
and forth while the orchestra
tunes up beneath the seats.

Look, my friend says, I'm in
heaven, I'm sorry
for your tears. Some of them
are for me, and I appreciate.
Thank you. That's love. But some
of them, let's face it, are
for you, so try not to be
stupid now and then go let
love lead to hatred. EAT
cheese. It's not a kidney.

In Monarch World

*At the end of the island, the monarchs grab the goldenrod
in headland dunes, dozens at once per stalk, talk about rusty
even when the wind and clouds come in and blow to horsehair,
and you think how that was while the hemisphere held its storms
in in its open cloak full of yo-yos, stolen clocks, mechanical birds,
and the secret smile is that we all know this place will be snorkeled.*

What are you? Houses go by on the backs of trucks.
The sideways silos of the septic trucks come to tap tap tap.
The more distant you get from the roofers at work
for the rich, the lazier the sounds of hammers.
De-peopled more and more itself, the beach shows
its long stripes, its blacks and tans gathering,
the fewer and fewer footprints to rye, no meat.

In the middle of all the sunbaked neo-realism of empty beaches, somebody had their ducks on a leash, bills forward straining like dogs who see other dogs who are full of play across the fields. Who are these people? What religion do they practice? Do they play recorders and tin whistles together? Do they blare Jethro Tull?

Free those ducks. We've been wandering in haze since medieval life, and who dosed us, the war of the roses? Two more miles of solitude, a truck parked on the sand, the fishing rods larger than any I have seen surf fishing, bolted into the sand like tent pegs, the lines way out. A dumbass can sit like a king by a cooler. He would shoot a tuna with a bazooka if he could, and the whole thing war and peace.

Acknowledgments

The early poem "For George Romero" appeared in *The Best of Lady Churchill's Rosebud Wristlet*, edited by Gavin Grant and Kelly Link, and the early poem "For William Morris" appeared in the deceased online journal *Nidus*, while "Cowardly Couplets" appeared in *Tuesday: an Art Project*. Most of the other poems here originally appeared in my first four books, *Ascension Days* (Del Sol Press, 2007), *Friends with Dogs* (Sheep Meadow Press, 2016), *Arsonville* (New Issues Poetry and Prose 2016), and *Barbarian Seasons* (MadHat Press, 2020). I am grateful to the editors and publishers of these books. Some poems that were originally parts of sequences appear as individual poems here. Thank you, Sabrina Blair, Marc Vincenz, Robert LeBlanc, David Rivard, Joseph Lease, Donald Revell, Robert Pinsky, Stuart Dischell, Alan Shapiro, Tanya Larkin, Stephanie Burt, Megan Breiseth, Tod Edgerton, Chloe Veylit, Donald Langosy, Dorothea Lasky, Tom Yuill, Natalie Reitano and Jordan Davis for helping me think about this selection as I worked on it. Special gratitude to Fred Chappell here.

About the Author

DAVID BLAIR grew up in Pittsburgh, Pennsylvania. He is the author of four earlier collections of poetry, *Ascension Days, Arsonville, Friends with Dogs*, and *Barbarian Seasons*, which, like his first collection of essays, *Walk Around: Essays on Poetry and Place*, is available from MadHat Press. Blair has degrees from Fordham University and the University of North Carolina at Greensboro. He lives with his wife and daughter in Somerville, Massachusetts, and he teaches poetry in the MFA Writing Program at the University of New Hampshire.

www.ingramcontent.com/pod-product-compliance
Lightning Source LLC
Chambersburg PA
CBHW020359170426
43200CB00005B/223